Bridgwater and the River Parrett

IN OLD PHOTOGRAPHS

Bridgwater and the River Parrett

IN OLD PHOTOGRAPHS

Compiled by ROD FITZHUGH

Alan Sutton Publishing Limited
Phoenix Mill · Far Thrupp
Stroud · Gloucestershire

First published 1993

Copyright © Rod Fitzhugh 1993

**British Library Cataloguing
in Publication Data**

Bridgwater and the River Parrett in Old
Photographs
  I. Fitzhugh, Rod
  942.38

ISBN 0-7509-0518-2

Typeset in 9/10 Sabon.
Typesetting and origination by
Alan Sutton Publishing Limited.
Printed in Great Britain by
Redwood Books, Trowbridge.

Contents

Introduction

The River Parrett, with its source in the rolling hills of north Dorset, crosses the Somerset boundary at South Perrot and passes close to Merriott, South Petherton, and Muchelney, where it joins the River Isle. Just south of Langport the River Yeo flows in from the south-east. The River Tone has its confluence just south of Burrowbridge and the Parrett continues on into Bridgwater and then, in surprising winding fashion, to Dunball, Combwich, and Burnham-on-Sea, before emerging into the Severn estuary in Bridgwater Bay, a total distance from source to sea of between thirty-five and forty miles.

The combination of a winding course with its bore and neap tides mean that as a waterway the Parrett has always been a potential hazard for shipping, navigable only to Bridgwater by the larger 400 to 500 ton vessels, and as far as Langport and Ilchester by barge using the Tone, Yeo and Isle and the Langport to Westport canal.

There is evidence for use of the Parrett from the Bronze Age through to the time of the Phoenicians, Romans, Saxons, Vikings, and Normans, and there were crossing points at Combwich, Crowpill and Bridgwater. It was not until the year 1200, however, and the grant of charters to Bridgwater, the building of the castle and of the first stone bridge, that the town developed as a trading port. By 1300 merchant trading brought into Bridgwater wine from France and exported corn, peas and beans to Ireland, France and Spain. By the 1400s the port was thriving, with wine imports and cloth exports from Somerset and Dorset to France and Spain. The Bristol Channel ports became accustomed to ships carrying cargo to and from Bridgwater, and the wharves in the nearby towns and villages with transfer to or from smaller craft – barges and so on – or the horse-drawn carts that provided the distribution network. By 1500 Bridgwater was the largest port in Somerset, its merchants selling agricultural produce to Ireland and hides to Spain, and using the ships for increased trade with the other Bristol Channel ports. Coal, timber, iron and millstones were imported, and although the cloth trade diminished throughout the sixteenth and seventeenth centuries trade actually improved, salt becoming an important cargo and Portugal being added to the trading nations.

The Bridgwater dry dock, built in 1743 for the repair, maintenance and building of ships, was a further incentive to ship owners to use the port. Over forty ships were built in the various shipyards along the river banks, creeks and pills during the eighteenth century, and the establishment of new industries producing bricks created a further increase in river and dock traffic.

The nineteenth century saw the Parrett at its peak, Bridgwater by then the leading industrial town in Somerset, with firms like Watsons, Luer and Company, David Williams, William Lowther, John Gough and F.J. Carver launching some 140 ships from their respective yards. Ships tied up at the wharves along the river, in town, village or countryside, as it was not until 1841 that the Bridgwater docks were opened. The excavated soil was piled on the north side and in time became known as 'the mump', a small part of which remains today.

The Bridgwater and Taunton Canal was extended to run into the western end of the docks, and the river and canal became linked. Local firms like Sully's, Axfords, Havilands and Stuckey and Bagehot of Langport became prominent ship owners, and by 1880 it was recorded that a quarter of a million tons of goods had been brought in during the previous twelve months. From sixteen brick and tile yards over twenty-four million bricks were exported downriver during the 1890s.

After so many centuries it was perhaps surprising that within twenty years the shipping trade had so drastically declined. The opening of the Severn Tunnel in 1886 led to the railway's being extended into Somerset and Dorset and then throughout the West Country. The waterways could not compete for goods traffic with the speed and penetration of the rail network, and there were financial losses in the docks. River wharves, starved of trade, started to close. Competition from the railways was coupled with the decline in the brick industry, which failed to mechanize and found the traditional 'Bath brick' outsold by other detergents and cleaning agents. Petroleum took over from coal and larger ships were berthing in larger and more accessible ports, so it was inevitable that shipping on the Parrett was nearing its end. Bridgwater docks finally closed on 31 July 1971, only being kept open so long for the sake of small trading craft. With the exception of trade at Dunball and Combwich, the River Parrett was reverting to pre-Bronze Age years. The wooden pillars against which the schooners, barques, and other tall-masted ships had once tied up were slowly sinking in the mud, their remains and the occasional ribs of a hulk a skeletal reminder of days gone by, the windowless ruin of Ware's warehouse the sightless skull of the cadaver of a once active river. The weeds and ruins were signs of dereliction and defeat.

But is the phoenix now rising? The Bridgwater docks, cleared of decades of rubbish, have been developed as a marina which will, hopefully, attract small craft to its moorings once the Bridgwater and Taunton Canal, now almost restored, is opened into the docks for pleasure boating. The Blake Museum displays all aspects of the heritage and history of the river, and a museum to the brickyard industry is in course of construction. The exciting and imaginative prospect of a barrage across the river poses many problems and sadly may be only a dream, but would create an inland waterway to rival the Broads of Norfolk. Perhaps from the demise of the River Parrett serving a trading port, is slowly rising the river as a source of pleasure for the leisure-time benefit of generations to come, and a constant reminder of the glories of the past.

Rod Fitzhugh

SECTION ONE
The Estuary

Flatholme lighthouse, *c*. 1917. During the hours of darkness, or in fog and gales, Flatholme lighthouse was a welcome sight on the Bristol Channel coastline. By its light mariners could navigate their vessels clear of the dangerous reefs, sandbanks and rocks.

Stolford 'mud-horse' *c.* 1910. As the tide recedes in Bridgwater Bay the Sellick family of Stolford take their 'mud-horse' on to Stert flats for the two-mile journey to their fishing nets strung between elm stakes. The 'mud-horse', made from a rectangular elm frame on a ski-shaped base, carried a large wicker basket and was propelled by leaning over the back of the frame and pushing hard against the deep grey mud. Having collected the bass, skate, shrimps, eels, sprats, sole and other fish from the nets, it was imperative that the return journey was started as soon as the tide turned, as in minutes the nets were covered by sometimes 20 ft of sea. The family continues the fishing tradition to this day.

BURNHAM & CARDIFF

New Fast "SHERBRO" Steamer

SHORTEST and CHEAPEST Route for GOODS & PASSENGERS to and from SOUTH WALES
The SOUTH & WEST of ENGLAND SOMERSETSHIRE DORSETSHIRE SOUTHAMPTON BOURNEMOUTH POOLE
PORTSMOUTH ISLE of WIGHT The CHANNEL ISLANDS and FRANCE via SOUTHAMPTON

The twin-funnelled wooden paddle-steamer *Sherbro*, built in 1870 by John White of Cowes, was used between May 1884 and 1886 on the Burnham-on-Sea to Cardiff ferry route, and then on cruises from Cardiff to Weston-super-Mare, Watchet, Lynmouth and Ilfracombe until 1888. Some years after Burnham-on-Sea jetty, situated alongside the slipway, ceased to be used by excursion vessels because of the build-up of silt and the dilapidated and dangerous pier timbers.

Brean Down ferry, one boat awaiting customers and the second bringing ashore four passengers. The crossing of the River Axe from Brean Down to Uphill by these small ferry boats saved a journey of several miles inland via Lympsham.

Brean Down, looking towards Uphill.

Brean Down from the south, showing a thatched cottage and stables, with two little girls posing for the cameraman. Brean Down is now managed by the National Trust as a bird sanctuary and is well known for its natural history, archaeological remains and as a scene of outstanding natural beauty. It was from Brean Down in May 1897 that Marconi and George Kemp transmitted and received the first wireless messages across water.

The fear of invasion by France prompted the utilization of four acres of land for the building of Brean Down Fort in 1862, one of four such forts across the Bristol Channel. Brean Down fort was developed with adjoining barracks and buildings and armed with cannons and guns, gunpowder and shot. Between 1905 and 1939 the fort was the more peaceful site of a café, but during the Second World War returned to war-time mode, being re-armed with guns and searchlights. Brean Down, 320 ft high, has always been a landmark for shipping using the ports of the Bristol Channel and an ideal vantage point for tourists, as well as the military, for watching the comings and goings of vessels.

Stolford, 1912. While the River Parrett is well known for its salmon fishing, other large 'fish' have been landed from or stranded by its waters. In 1884 and 1888 'Royal' sturgeon were caught weighing in at 2½ cwt, and later exhibited at Pople & Porters' fish and poultry shop in High Street, Bridgwater. In 1880, 1885 and 1913 porpoise of over one hundredweight were taken from the Parrett, a school also being sighted off Burnham-on-Sea in 1888. A large whale washed ashore at Combwich in the 1860s, and the bottle-nosed whale shown in this photograph beached itself on 27 September 1912 having been seen lashing around in the mud before the tide receded. Measured at some 19 ft in length and weighing between three and four tons, it was buried in the vicinity, but not before hundreds of people had flocked to see such a rare event.

Trows *Sarah* and *Eliza*, *c.* 1936. Many of the River Severn trows ended their days minus masts and rigging and used as cargo-carrying barges or lighters. *Eliza*, built in 1865 at Runcorn, was registered at Bridgwater in 1898. The *Sarah* was built in Framilode, Gloucestershire and registered at Bridgwater in 1923. Both are shown here at Bristol in their less glamorous barge style. *Sarah* was finally wrecked in 1947, and *Eliza* was broken up some two years later.

Uphill Wharf in around 1936 was the final resting place of three well known local vessels. To the right is the *Norah*, a Severn trow built by John Gough of Bridgwater in 1868 and used for many years in the Bristol corn trade. She was finally owned by Captain Smart, who used her as a house-boat before she was given a Viking funeral in 1939. In the middle is the 1883 Goole-built ketch, *Daisy*, owned by Captain Crockey, a retired seafarer who lived on the craft whilst she was laid up at Uphill. Bought for £5 in June 1938 by H. Penfold of Hewish, the hulk was filled with tyres and set alight, only her ironwork being salvaged. To the left is the 1890 ketch *R. Passmore*, built at Burton Stather and purchased as a hulk in 1938 for £4 2s 6d.

SECTION TWO
Burnham-on-Sea

Constructed of Canadian teak in 1832, this 36 ft high Burnham lighthouse stands on stilts on the sands and is unique in this country. The Local Authority maintains the structure now, having assumed responsibility from Trinity House when it became redundant in 1969.

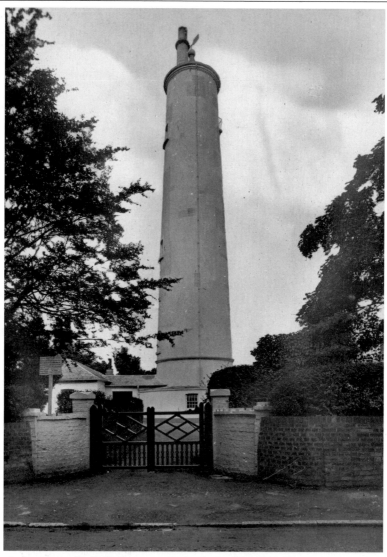

Also built in 1832, this lighthouse is 91 ft above the high water mark. Both have a broad red line down the frontage and were built on the recommendation of Lt Henry Mongles Denham RN, who, having surveyed the entrance to the Bristol Channel, saw the need for such structures to ensure safe navigation off Burnham. This particular lighthouse was opened to the public before the First World War from 9.30 a.m. to one hour before sunset. Safe passage through the dangerous sandbanks obstructing the narrow entrance to the estuary required the pilot to bring his vessel into a position where the high light appeared directly above the low light. The latter gave out a red and white signal, while the high light shone with a plain white light for three minutes then darkened shutters obscured the light for 35 seconds. Captains thus had the different presentations of both lighthouses to effect correct navigation.

High and dry off Burnham-on-Sea in 1937, the ketch *Bessie Ellen*, built at Plymouth in 1907, had no option but to await the next tide to be refloated and to resume her journey. It is believed that this vessel is now with Danish owners, undergoing extensive restoration, and has been re-named *Forsoget*. If this is right it will be a joy to see her as she was when launched and was a familiar sight off Burnham shores.

This picture from the Burnham slipway shows one of the many Burnham pilot boats designed and built double-ended, two-masted and with bowsprit. These curved-sided, clinker boats would take the pilot out into the estuary in all weathers to give help to ketches waiting to be brought up river on the incoming tide. Other pilot cutters providing identical service included the *Polly*, *Sunbeam* and *Star of the Sea*.

This was a familiar scene from the sea-front at Burnham-on-Sea at the turn of the century. A tugboat tows the three-masted topsail schooner *Gaca* as the steamship *Bauto* makes headway in the estuary.

Burnham from the Sea.

Flatners were double-ended, open boats built in two sizes and ideal for use on the muddy banks of the tidal River Parrett. The 19 ft 6 in *Gore* is shown here off Burnham-on-Sea with her sprit-sail rig catching the prevailing wind. Two men were required to sail the craft, one to control the rudder and mainsheet, the other to control the jibsheet and forward dagger board. Flatners were constructed of tongued and grooved planks on a timber frame, and covered inside and outside with tar. A bolt and chain was used for towing, and they were used throughout the year for fishing in the river or estuary and for sea going. Henry Wilkins of Combwich and H.J. Kimber of Highbridge were the well known builders of this craft, as well as the 16 ft *Bay*. A smaller version of these vessels, usually about 15 ft in length, was used on the rhines and ditches for carrying bundles or 'bolts' of harvested withies.

P. & A. Campbells' White Funnel Fleet steel paddle-steamer *Waverley*, built in 1885 by H. McIntyre & Co. of Paisley, is seen here taking on passengers at Burnham-on-Sea pier in 1908. These boat excursions sailed the Bristol Channel to South Wales, the coast of Somerset and North Devon, the Holms, Lundy Island, and even as far as Bude and Tenby. Although competition with other companies was considerable, by the 1920s the White Funnel Fleet had the lead. The *Waverley* was broken up in 1921 but the remaining paddle-steamers were used for carrying troops and for mine-sweeping during the Second World War, changing names for security reasons as had happened between 1914 and 1918.

The landing-slip constructed between September 1857 and 3 May 1858, when the Burnham extension of the Somerset Central Railway was opened. The mooring piles alongside the jetty, together with the parallel line opposite, enabled ships to tie alongside the pier. To the left foreground is the sluice-gate necessary to control the silt within the berth. Trucks would be pulled up the 1-in-23 gradient by wire rope attached through a ring from the pierhead to the nearby station. It was from this pier that Burnham lifeboat was launched on a rail bogie. In the background to the left is the steam paddle-tug *Petrel* awaiting high tide to tow several loaded vessels up river as far as Bridgwater.

The Norwegian barque *Nornen*, built in 1876, dragged her anchors while moored in Lundy Roads during a storm on 2 March 1897. With snow falling, high winds and her sails in tatters she was driven ashore at Berrow Flats. The Burnham lifeboat, the *John Godfrey Morris*, was launched with a thirteen man crew using her ten oars, but the *Nornen* had beached and the crew was safe. The coxswain Mr Alfred Hunt landed his crew and one dog at Burnham-on-Sea, where they were looked after by the Shipwrecked Mariners' Society. Attempts were made to lighten her, but she was stuck fast and was later broken up on the beach. To this day her remains are visible when currents and shifting sands reveal the wreck at low tide near to Berrow church.

The 34 ft water-ballast lifeboat *John Godfrey Morris* on the rail bogie from which she was launched at Burnham-on-Sea on 13 December 1887, thus replacing the *Cheltenham*. She continued in service until December 1902, when she was superseded by the *Philip Beach*, a Liverpool-type lifeboat.

The 35 ft lifeboat *Philip Beach* arrived at Burnham-on-Sea on 16 December 1902, and during service until 1930 saved at least five lives, later being sold for yacht conversion. This photograph pictures the many helpers prepared to haul the boat, stern first, up the steep slipway to the lifeboat house on her rail bogie. How many men would wear a suit and hat while walking the beach and pier? How fashions change.

The listing steamship *Pelle* is towed carefully into port by the tugboat *Rexford*, her deck cargo probably having shifted during a rough passage at sea.

The *Pelle* is safely moored in the river, her port list plainly visible.

Onlookers watch and wait for the next tide as the safely anchored *Borderdene*, a small Bridgwater-registered steamship built in 1913, lies high and dry at Burnham.

The Highbridge-owned tugboat *Rexford* off Burnham, no doubt floated off on the next incoming tide.

An old railway coach on Burnham pierhead known as the 'Cathedral' was used by and provided food and comfort for the pilots and seamen of Burnham and Bridgwater. With a fixed table and a coal stove heated by fuel from local coal boats, the building served its purpose until it was replaced in 1938 by a new shelter, lit and heated by gas. The following well known local names appear in the picture above: Mr Green (station master), W. Press, Captain Hunt, pilots Fred (Tich) King, J. King and T. Surfield, E. Brewer, ? Brewer. Among the front row are: Tom Parsons, G. Parsons, George Clapp and Jud Thomas.

Highbridge

The Russian barquentine *Mercator*, 370 tons and 141 ft long, was built at Haynaech in 1895 and is here shown at the Highbridge wharf unloading her cargo of timber from Archangel in September 1903. The decorative 'ports' were often painted on sailing ships of this period, as a reminder of days when merchant shipping carried cannon for defence. The last cargo ship brought timber to this wharf in 1948.

A foreign steamer discharges her cargo at Highbridge wharf.

A turn of the century study of ketches and trows, sail and spars. In the foreground is the ketch *Galley* with, behind, the Severn trow *Norah*, built at Bridgwater by John Gough in 1868. The *Norah* was to become a hulk at Uphill in the 1930s and was burnt in 1939.

A large three-masted barque makes a majestic sight moored alongside Highbridge wharf with a ketch both fore and aft. Wine was imported; cheese and skimmed milk were exported to South Wales for the Caerphilly cheese.

The steamship *Julia*, owned by the Somerset & Dorset Joint Railway Company, was built in 1904 at Woolston and was a sister ship to the steamship *Radstock*. Having unloaded her coal at Highbridge wharf, she is seen here with her boat stowed on the hatches ready to catch the next tide. After thirty years she was broken up in 1934.

The Oslo-registered steamship *Primula* in the River Brue in 1938. This picture clearly shows the size of ships using Highbridge wharf, vessels stacked high with Scandinavian timber. Highbridge wharf was closed to shipping in 1949.

The steamship *Bertha* discharging her cargo at Highbridge wharf, the timber stacked high above the main deck held in place with numerous uprights. Clearly shown are her own booms, in use unloading the wood without need for shore-based cranes.

The steamship *Julia* bedecked with flags and bunting and displaying her signals as she makes her way to Highbridge wharf on 6 July 1904, her maiden voyage. Dignitaries and company staff line the decks. She traded regularly from this port until she was broken up in 1934.

This 1½ ton steam-operated hydraulic lifting-crane was built in 1891, numbered 2, and belonged to the Somerset & Dorset Joint Railway Company. It is seen here working alongside Highbridge wharf, mounted and running on broad gauge track. To the right is the 1877 Bridgwater-registered steamship *Alpha*, also owned by the S&DJR and broken up in 1925.

The steamship *Leopard*, registered in Bridgwater and again owned by the Somerset & Dorset Joint Railway Company, was built in Bristol in 1861 and broken up in 1911.

An unusual view taken in 1937 from the quayside at Highbridge wharf, with the Bridgwater-registered ketch *Sunshine* alongside and the main and aft hatch, ventilator, discharging gaff, main and mizzen masts and steering wheel all clearly visible.

Sunshine photographed looking forward, her bowsprit clearly visible.

The steamship *Elemore* of Bristol alongside Highbridge wharf having unloaded a cargo of coal from South Wales by steam crane. Now sitting light in the river, her winch would have been used to stow her tender boat on deck before sailing on the next tide.

The 1874 brigantine *Livonia* at Highbridge wharf, where the volume of trade is obvious from the five vessels, sail and steam, loading and unloading their cargo. Highbridge saw imports of flour, coal, timber and iron rails, and exported bricks. With hindsight, we now know that trade had peaked and at the time of this photograph (*c.* 1910) was already in decline.

The hulk of the ketch *Marian* disintegrating on the mud in Highbridge River. Built in 1869 by John Gough of Bridgwater, she was finally given a Viking funeral and was deliberately burnt in 1939.

The Bridgwater-built ketch *Fanny Jane* aground at Highbridge Pill, awaiting the next tide to discharge her cargo. The very rapid rise and fall of the tide made it easy to misjudge the time available for berthing, and many boats suffered from a long wait before being refloated.

SECTION FOUR

Combwich

The Pill. Combwich.

Bridgwater's famous and only surviving ketch *Irene*, here moored at Combwich Pill, and, behind, the ketch *Woodcock*, built in Barnstaple by W.S. Kelly in 1895. Combwich was not only a trading port for many centuries, but was also known for the use made by local fishermen of dipping nets from 'flatners', 16 or 19 ft long, flat-bottomed, double-ended boats with no keel. Henry Wilkins of Combwich was reputed to have built the best of these local craft, which could be used throughout the year and were sometimes equipped with a sail. They were a familiar sight to members of the local older generation.

The rather forlorn sight of the ketch *New Design*, built at Bridgwater in 1871 by John Gough, at Combwich Pill prior to sale, after which she was laid up at Bristol Bridge until 1946 and finally hulked in 1951. Her name derived from her construction with only half the usual number of ribs but of twice the usual thickness. Interestingly, she shows an unsheltered open wheel and a whale-backed lavatory-box on her starboard side.

West End, Combwich, *c.* 1909.

The ketch *Woodcock*, built in Plymouth in 1895, was a regular sight at Combwich. She is pictured here on a calm high tide as her boat is lifted on board to be secured to the hatches under the main boom prior to sailing, her discharging gaff lowered to deck.

The sad sight of the 1867 Bridgwater-built trow *Severn*, hulked and dilapidated in her final resting place at Combwich Pill. As tides rose and fell over the years, her timbers sank deeper into the mud, and she slowly disintegrated until nothing was left. The bowsprit of the *Irene* is visible behind her.

Seen here at Combwich Pill, the Bristol-registered ketch *Emily*, owned by Combwich & District Farmers' Association, was built at Chepstow in 1895 and foundered in the Bristol Channel. On Saturday 22 September 1934, while laden with coal, she capsized off Flat Holm during rough seas on a voyage to Bridgwater. Captain Thomas Granter of Combwich and deckhand Harry Davis of Polden Street, Bridgwater survived, but the mate, Reginald Phelps of Bridgwater, went down with the doomed ketch.

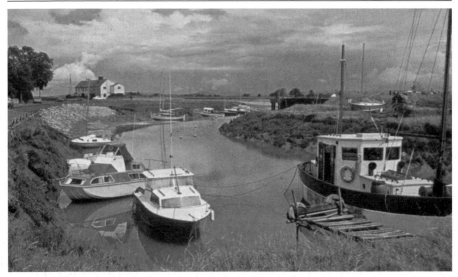

A more modern view of Combwich Pill. Leisure craft have taken the place of ketches and schooners. To the right is the Port of Bridgwater's converted wooden motor trawler *Bridgwater Castle*. Built in 1945 at Bideford as the *Anncliveian* and later called *Huntley Castle*, the re-named *Bridgwater Castle* is now used for the inspection of buoys in the mouth of the River Parrett as well as general river maintenance. For some years she was moored either in the Pill or beached on the opposite bank of the River Parrett at Pawlett Hams.

The 1878 Salcombe-built ketch *Sarah Jane* alongside Combwich Quay. Her discharging gaff pulled up on her main mast shows clearly, and on the 'skid' a man with an empty basket waits to fill it with coal before it is swung out of the hold and unhooked. The ketch would then be loaded with bricks and tiles before her departure. The *Sarah Jane* was wrecked off Ilfracombe during the First World War.

The Bridgwater ketch *Squirrel*, built in 1882 by F.J. Carver of East Quay, moored at Combwich Pill. This unusual picture, looking aft from the main hatch, shows the whale-back toilet shelter, aft hatch and canvas hatch-cover, skylight, ventilator, and, on the left, the fresh drinking water tank with two lifebelts secured on top. The end of the main boom with its heavy treble block shows clearly the mizzen gaff resting on the mizzen boom and secured with a double block attached to the stern rail. The open wheel had no shelter against the elements and sailors at the helm suffered from the lack of protection.

A horse and cart belonging to the Combwich & District Farmers' Association in the local fields with its keeper. The Association owned a number of sailing vessels used regularly over the years by the farming communities to the east of the Quantock Hills who traded out of Combwich with corn and produce, returning with coal and coke. The last Combwich-owned craft was the ketch *Emily* which was lost off Flat Holm on 22 September 1934 while bringing coal from Lydney for the Farmers' Association.

The motor vessel *Seatern* of Seaway Coasters Ltd unloading cargo at Combwich for transportation by road to the Hinkley Point Atomic Power Station. This modern harbour installation, with its heavy duty lifting crane belonging to Babcock & Wilcox Ltd, was specially constructed to bring in cargo by ship and avoid the constant road transportation problems from more distant ports of 'abnormal loads'.

Unrecognizable today, the Anchor Inn was a favourite hostelry for seamen visiting Combwich Pill. At the time of this photograph the Licensee was William Manchip, who provided 'Luncheons, Teas and all classes of Refreshments', which were no doubt very welcome after the hardship of long hours at sea in open vessels with little or no protection against the notoriously inclement weather of the Bristol Channel.

In 1878 John Gough of Bridgwater built this beautiful schooner, appropriately named *Princess of Thule*, shown here moored at Combwich in around 1910 with gang plank in position for loading and unloading. In the distance, visible below her bowsprit, is the now demolished White House public house, which was on the east side of the River Parrett at Pawlett Hams. This was the crossing-point over the Parrett for pilgrims en route to Glastonbury, who used either stepping stones at low tide or, in later years, a ferry. The causeway, or 'cassy' as it was known, was still being crossed by horse-drawn wagons at the turn of the century but, later, ferry boats transported sheep, cattle and foot passengers. This particular crossing saved miles of travel for people and animals alike since the nearest alternative was as far away as Bridgwater.

Dunball.

The main lines of the Great Western Railway Company and the tracks running into Dunball Wharf. Imports of coal, timber, sand and gravel were unloaded here for transportation elsewhere by rail. Built in 1844 as a horse-worked tramway, in November 1869 the tracks were converted for steam locomotives using both standard and broad gauge track, and in May 1892 to standard gauge only. Dunball wharf was extended in 1874 with an additional branch, over which a 5 m.p.h. speed limit was imposed. The author remembers how as recently as the 1950s a man with a red flag would halt road traffic on the main A38 Bristol to Bridgwater road when a train with a maximum of twenty-five wagons was crossing. The branch line, of some 792 yd in length, was closed on 19 March 1962.

On Saturday 16 July 1921 the steamship *Tender*, belonging to Messrs Sully & Co. of Bridgwater, heeled over while being berthed at Dunball wharf with a cargo of coal from Lydney, South Wales. It was not until the following Friday that a tug from Cardiff righted the vessel, a portion of coal having been discharged into barges, by placing empty casks into the hold to permit her being towed stern up and righted on the ebb tide. No damage was caused by the incident and she continued trading until broken up in 1942, then sixty-nine years old and in almost constant use since her launch.

The unusual four-masted vessel *Laanemar of Tallinn* at Dunball wharf in 1936 after discharging her cargo of timber from Scandinavia.

The steamship *Ronny* lists to starboard, having run aground off Dunball on a falling tide. A ropeman in the bow appears about to throw a line ashore. This would be attached to a heavier rope and hauled to the bank to enable the ship to be made secure and thus avoid the possibility of her capsizing as the water level receded further.

This delightful picture taken at Dunball in 1933 shows seventeen intrepid men just prior to their five-mile swim from Dunball to the Town Bridge in Bridgwater. The men's full length swimming costumes and skull caps were high fashion at the time!

The Stockholm-registered steamship *Hebe* discharging timber alongside Dunball wharf in July 1938. The mobile steam cranes operating on track alongside the wharf were used to load to and from waiting railway trucks.

The graceful ketch *Emma Louise*, built in 1883 by William Westacott of Barnstaple, moored alongside Dunball wharf. After the First World War she was owned by the Rawle family of Minehead and traded between the Bristol Channel ports for many years. She was still in commission in 1948. With a jib boom and bowsprit, she carried a fine figurehead which has been preserved and can be seen at the North Devon Maritime Museum.

The three-masted steamship *Freza* of Kalman unloads her cargo of timber at Dunball wharf in 1948, with steam cranes and saddle-tank locomotive alongside.

While a steam crane unloads a cargo of timber at Dunball wharf in the 1930s, a member of the crew occupies his time painting the hull of this Hamburg vessel. He is seated on a trestle suspended from the bow. The wharf was also used extensively for the discharge of coal shipped from South Wales to be distributed throughout the West of England by railway.

The Danish steamship *Olga* in difficulty off Dunball wharf. Having discharged her cargo of timber from Scandinavia, the pilot misjudged the tide and ran aground. A twelve hour wait for the next high tide was needed to refloat the vessel.

The steamship *Kajsa Christensen* in difficulty at Dunball wharf, having grounded in mid-river on an ebb tide. Heavily laden with timber from Scandinavia stacked high above her decks, she lists to port at a precarious angle.

She was able to berth safely on the following tide, however, and safely discharge her cargo.

The trow *Charles* owned by Mr J.C. Hunt, shipbroker of Bridgwater, became a total wreck on Monday 19 November 1906 while bringing coal from Cardiff. The vessel was brought up river by Captain William Britton on the evening tide and the anchor was dropped off Dunball, but with a strong wind and tide the anchor chain fouled the windlass, causing the vessel's stem to collide with the quay wall, damaging her bows. Although two barges of coal were removed on the following day, the remainder of her cargo was lost. The cargo was fully insured but the trow was only covered for a small sum.

The labour-intensive occupation of quarrying stone with not a machine in sight at the Puriton Quarry of John Board & Co. Ltd. The layers of stone on the right were dug out by hand and loaded on to wheelbarrows. Workers had to push heavy wheelbarrows across the planks, some 18 in wide and about 35 ft long, supported by wooden trestles about 30 ft above the floor of the quarry. The stone was used for cement and for the limekilns until they were closed in 1973.

The *Prudence* was a typical Bristol Channel trow used for the transportation of coal from Cardiff, Newport and Lydney to Bristol, Avonmouth, and ports on the River Parrett. Seen here in 1910 at Dunball wharf, *Prudence* was built in 1822 at Beathall, Shropshire in typical ketch style. Steered with a tiller, she had an open hold with no hatches but with canvas side-cloths in the absence of bulwarks except around her bow and stern quarters. As a result she was vulnerable in heavy seas and was used mainly in coastal waters. The small boat below her stern was reputedly used by one Jessie Ware, who would place a lantern on Dunball Point for the benefit of vessels using the river in darkness.

SECTION SIX
River Scene

Built in 1901 by William Hurd of Chepstow, and Bridgwater-registered, the ketch *Edith* is seen here berthed alongside Chilton Trinity Brickyard while she is loaded with bricks and tiles. Originally built as an open Severn trow, this photograph clearly shows the canvas side-cloths amid the bulwarks to the bow and stern typical of the trow. On 13 July 1903, while captained by Mr M. Warren of Bridgwater, the *Edith* collided with the landing stage at Brean Down Quarries during a raging gale and turned completely on her side. Because of the considerable damage sustained she had to be towed to Bridgwater for repair. On 8 July 1914 she went aground on the bank opposite the Bridgwater Hospital but was refloated on the evening tide without damage. She was motorized in 1927 and registered as 'unwanted' in 1960.

How not to secure your vessel! Built in 1867 by John Gough of Bridgwater, the 60 ton ketch *Fame* lies capsized alongside the original Chilton Trinity Brickyard of the Somerset Trading Company. She was successfully refloated this time, but finally ran aground on the east bank of the River Parrett above Dunball wharf, where her remains are still visible. In the background is the 120 ft brickyard chimney constructed with 85,000 bricks which was eventually demolished on the 30 December 1931 by the Bridgwater firm of Messrs Pollard & Sons.

The Somerset Trading Company used postcards to display its premises at Chilton Tile Factory. The reverse of this card advertises its products, namely Bath Bricks and Bath Brick Powder. The tall chimney was demolished on 30 December 1931, when timbers at the base were saturated with oil and tar. After being alight for just five minutes, the burning timbers gave way and the stack fell within five feet of its intended direction.

The Bridgwater-registered ketch *Emily*, in superb photographic profile, in full sail on the River Parrett. She foundered east of Flat Holm in 1934. The Captain, Thomas Granter of Combwich, and Harry Davis of Bridgwater were able to board a dinghy, but the mate, Reginald Phelps of Bridgwater, tragically died.

The steam paddle-tug *Petrel* hauling the schooner *Rosevean* past Crowpill on a rising tide in around 1865. *Petrel* was built in 1863 at Low Walker. *Rosevean* was built at Scilly in 1847 and ended her days in 1906 hulked on the banks of the River Parrett.

The tidal bore sweeping up river at Saltlands, Bridgwater in 1913, with the 1858 ketch *Fanny Jane*, built by John Gough of Bridgwater, securely moored at Colthurst Symons wharf. To the left is the wharf of John Symons & Co. Ltd, where scouring bricks imprinted with the name 'Bridgwater Bath Brick Company' were made.

On a Tuesday in late November 1921 the steamship *Martha* collided with the ketch *Champion* at Dunball wharf while being towed up river. Later, while opposite the premises of the Parrett Bath Brick Co., the *Martha* and the two towing tugs went aground, one of the tugs being jammed against the bank. On the morning tide the *Martha* swung across the river and completely blocked it to all other vessels. Some of her cargo was removed and on the Wednesday night she was floated up river to Saltlands, where she grounded yet again! On Thursday she was refloated and, safely this time, proceeded into the docks where her cargo was discharged. Records indicate that the SS *Martha* was manned by a German captain and crew and that despite all these mishaps she sustained no damage, no doubt to the relief of shipbrokers Messrs Charles Hunt & Co. of Bridgwater.

This chilly scene, taken on 1 January 1880, shows the severity of the winter when it was possible to walk across the Saltlands area of the frozen River Parrett at Bridgwater. On the left is the schooner *Octavius*, built only two years earlier by F.J. Carver & Son of Bridgwater; next is the steam barge *Alpha*, built in 1877 and broken up in 1925; an unknown smack and a ketch complete the picture.

The *GBS*, a large iron barque named after George Bryant Sully, one of the well known members of the Bridgwater family of coal importers. Built in 1876 at Sunderland, this 545 ton barque was 164 ft in length but considered uneconomic, so she was sold by Sully & Co. in 1882 and later re-named *West Australian* of London. The location of this photograph is unknown.

Nearing Bridgwater docks on 8 November 1908, the Norwegian three-masted brigantine *Eidsvold* of Frederickstadt was wrecked. The vessel of 313 tons was heavily laden with deal boards from Norway for Messrs George Hooper & Co. Ltd, timber importers of Bridgwater. On reaching the mouth of the Parrett she was taken in tow by the *Bonita* and *Victor*, but, while only 200 yd short of the docks, an easterly wind cut the tide down to two feet, which caused the vessel's bow to touch the west bank and the stern rope to part. The *Eidsvold* swung across the river and the stem embedded on the other side. Attempts were made to refloat her the following day to no avail, so deck cargo was taken off. She then sprang a leak and filled with water. A month and a day later she was auctioned as a wreck and was bought for the princely sum of £41 6s by a Mr Hurley of Bristol. She was emptied of her remaining cargo and then towed away by a Cardiff tug to be broken up by an Appledore shipbreaker. However, on the way to Appledore she made so much water she had to be taken into Penarth for safety.

The unladen ketch *Martin Luther*, built in 1847 at Cowes and owned by Fred Penberthy of Weston-super-Mare, makes her majestic way up the calm River Parrett under full sail.

To the left of this photograph is the Bridgwater Steam Towing Company's tug *Bonita*, under her master Captain Smart, in the process of taking in tow the Severn-decked trow *Duke of Wellington*, as well as an unknown smack. Up to six vessels would be taken in tow and brought up river, different boats being cast off at various ports on the way. The *Bonita* was sunk off Liverpool on 3 May 1941 by bombs from a German aircraft.

Alongside the bank of the river at the western end of Pawlett Hams, the White House Inn, last licensed in around 1911, was a familiar landmark to navigators on the Parrett until demolished in about 1930. This very early photograph was taken on a glass negative in around the 1850s with the then licensee Robert Wilkins standing outside. A causeway led down to the river bank, which afforded crossing on foot or saddled horse at low tide, or by ferry worked from Combwich.

The Sully & Co. steamship *Enid*, built in 1903 at Maryhill, makes her way up river on a fast flowing incoming tide to Bridgwater docks to unload her cargo of coal from South Wales. She was a familiar sight on the River Parrett during the 1940s and '50s until she was broken up in 1959.

On Thursday 16 October 1910 the ketch *Arthur* of Bridgwater was being towed to her berth opposite the Parrett Bath Brick Co.'s yard. On being released from the tug the tow rope fouled its anchor as it was being lowered and, with a strong wind blowing, the *Arthur* went aground on the bank. When the tide receded she heeled over on her side, her masts parallel with the water. The next day, with ropes attached to her side and with the assistance of a Parrett barge floated under her masts, she was pulled into an upright position and was ready to sail again, having, quite remarkably, sustained little damage.

The topsail schooner *C.&F. Nurse* was built in 1900 by Lean of Falmouth for the Nurse family of Bridgwater and is seen here loading alongside the brickyard of John Board & Co. After the Second World War she was owned and commanded by Captain Kelly of Nether Stowey and was the last locally owned schooner. Subsequently she plied her trade as a barge under the name of *Enterprise* before being laid up in the Gloucestershire canal for some years and finally broken up in 1955.

Originally built as a two-masted schooner at Waterhuizen in 1915, the Poole-registered *Hanna* makes her way up river to Dunball in 1948 under her own auxiliary engine. This lovely boat was wrecked off Jersey in 1949 while on passage from Plymouth loaded with limestone.

On Saturday 27 August 1904, while being towed up the River Parrett with a cargo of wood from Westwick, the Norwegian barque *Punctum* went aground at Second Pound Field some 1½ miles below Bridgwater docks. Crowds gathered on the Sunday evening to watch tug boats pull her off on the high tide so that she could be taken into the dock.

What must have been a familiar sight in years past is shown in this photograph taken at Saltlands of the steam tug *Bonita* towing three ketches from Bridgwater towards the mouth of the Parrett. Left to right are the *Annie Christian*, *Spartan* and *Fanny Jane*.

On 28 August 1948 the ketch *Emily Barrett* went aground on a mudbank off Horsey Pill near Dunball. Built as a schooner in 1913 by the Duddon Shipbuilding Company of Cumberland, and named after a member of the Duddon family, she was said to be the last merchant sailing ship ever built. She served as the hulk for a barrage balloon in Falmouth harbour during the last war before being fitted with a new keel and keelson and re-rigged as a ketch, part of the work being carried out at Appledore. She was used extensively for the carrying of coal from Lydney and also for the carrying of bricks from Bridgwater.

The hulk of the *Biland*, built in 1865, of 451 tons, on the bank of the River Parrett.

For months all that was visible of the ketch *Trio* was her mast top! In March 1939, under Captain Warren of Bridgwater and on the ebb tide, she accidentally grounded on the edge of a mudbank known as 'Pursey's Mare' just north of Combwich, and as the tide receded the *Trio* fell over and proved a total loss. Built in 1877 at Jersey as a schooner, she later entered the ownership of the Escott family of Watchet and then the Slade family of Appledore, who re-rigged her as a ketch. It is worth a visit to the area at low tide when it is sometimes possible to see her few remains.

The schooner *Rosevean*, built in 1847 at Scilly, was hulked on the banks of the Parrett in 1906.

The difficulties of navigating the River Parrett could not be more clearly illustrated than in this view of the ketch-rigged Severn trow *Ark*, which has just run aground a mile below Bridgwater docks. Her small boat, which was always towed behind vessels in the river in anticipation of this kind of incident, would have been hastily sculled to deeper water. A kedge, or anchor, would have been dropped to enable the *Ark* to pull herself off. Ahead of the *Ark* is the 1858 Bridgwater-built ketch *Fanny Jane*, wrecked in 1963.

The three-masted *Ann Charlotte* brings timber to Bridgwater in July 1949.

The 500 ton Danish sailing vessel *N.P. Peterson* from Archangel, with a cargo of timber for Messrs Hooper & Co. of Bridgwater, arrived late on the morning tide of Saturday 7 September 1929 at Little Reach, about 1½ miles below Bridgwater Dock. While being towed by two tugs, she grounded on the bank and as the tide continued to recede she developed a decided list. Two barge-loads of timber had to be removed before she could be refloated on the night tide. However, after only 100 yd and in darkness she grounded on the flood tide on the opposite bank. A further 200 tons of cargo was removed, but it was not until a week later that she was finally refloated and able to sail on her way.

The suction dredger *Steep Holm* belonging to the Holms Sand & Gravel Company makes her way down river having discharged her cargo at Bridgwater docks.

The River Parrett at Little Reach with Hawkers Farm to the left. At high tide a barquentine uses her auxiliary power while outward bound, and a ketch, low in the water, makes her way up river. A steam tug is visible between them.

The Bristol-registered trow *Flora*, empty and aground on ice at 'Pondfields' during a severe winter. In the distance to the left can be seen Hawkers Farm, with the A38 Bristol to Bridgwater road on the right. In March 1909, while owned by Captain Webb of Dunball, the master of the *Flora* was tragically lost overboard during a gale off the Holms when she was being sailed from Bridgwater to Cardiff loaded with coal. Apparently her tiller swung round and knocked Captain William Britton of Bailey Street, Bridgwater into the sea. A gallant attempt to rescue him was made by the mate, Frederick Bawdrip, who lowered a boat to reach the mariner, but failed to bring on board the captain, who left a widow and nine children.

Bridgwater

On Saturday 7 September 1872 the schooner *Sam Weller*, built for the Bridgwater firm of Brown & Co., was launched from the Bridgwater shipbuilding yard of John Gough at Crowpill in the presence of a large number of spectators. This vessel only had a short lifespan, foundering in 1899. The two yards on her foremast clearly distinguish the schooner from the ketches familiar on the river and in the docks. The bulwark, when removed, allowed a plank to be inserted on her starboard side which facilitated the loading and unloading of cargo. To her outside is the ketch *Clare Felicia* of Caernarvon, built at Nevin in 1873.

One of the oldest and most important commercial firms in Bridgwater was that of Sully & Company, shipowners and coal factors. Thomas Sully, always interested in the shipping trade, was born in Watchet in 1767 and moved to Bridgwater soon after 1800, the larger port offering better facilities than his home town. He died in July 1824 and was buried in Watchet. He left his property, including his prize brigantine *Brothers*, in trust for the benefit of his children, and two years later his eldest son, also called Thomas and aged 23, started the business of Sully & Company.

The opening of the Bridgwater and Taunton Canal in 1827 enabled coal imported from South Wales to be distributed by barges to places along the waterway. With the construction of the Bridgwater docks in 1841 trade expanded further. The subsequent development by the Bristol & Exeter Railway of the wharves and sidings at Dunball led to the company's increasing its shipping fleet to meet the need for coal.

In June 1845 James Wood Sully, brother of Thomas, joined the firm, which became known as Thomas & J.W. Sully. In 1855 shipbroking was separated from the coal business, and George Bryant Sully, the eldest son of Thomas, operated in the name of 'Sully & Hurman'. In 1849 the partners had bought a third share in two Forest of Dean collieries, 'Parkend' and 'New Fancy', acquiring a further third interest from Thomas Nicholson of Lydney in 1858. They became the sole owners with the purchase of the final third in 1860 from Mr Trotter and traded as Parkend Coal Company. With the retirement of Thomas in 1860, J.W. Sully remained as sole proprietor, and the name of the firm was shortened to Sully & Co. Thomas Sully died in 1861, his son, George Bryant Sully, in Brussels in 1907, aged 76. The three sons of J.W. Sully, Thomas, John George and Richard Owen, entered the business.

In 1870 the Bristol & Exeter Railway brought tracks across the River Parrett to Bridgwater docks, and J.W. Sully, who was then living at Crowpill adjoining the docks, converted a large field next to his house into a railway yard so that coal could be discharged from vessels straight into railway trucks. To cope with the expansion of business John Sully bought 100 broad gauge railway wagons, the first privately owned trucks in the West Country. He also purchased the steamship *Bulldog*, the first such vessel owned at Bridgwater.

On 30 June 1876 J.W. Sully transferred all his interest in Sully & Co to his three sons, Thomas, John George and Richard Owen, but retained the Parkend Coal Company in his own name. Thomas died on 31 October 1877, aged 33, and was buried at Lydney. In 1880 the firm owned 300 rail wagons, 20 sailing ships and 2 steam boats, but in that year the collieries were sold as the existing seams were worked out and the cost of sinking lower seams would have been prohibitive. J.W. Sully died in 1886, aged 79, at Mount Radford, Bridgwater, the home of his son John.

The opening of the Severn Tunnel in 1886 led to a decline in shipping so the sailing vessels were reduced in number, but the rail wagons increased to over 600 in number and a third steamship, the *Welsh Prince*, was purchased to complement the *Bulldog* and *Tender*. GWR broad gauge became standard gauge, and in 1892 the Sully wagons were altered at Swindon. In 1894 John George Sully retired to live at Clevedon and Richard Owen Sully became managing director of the private

Employees of Sully & Co. rest on their shovels while the photographer captures the dirty and back-breaking task of unloading coal from the hold of the steamship *Crowpill* at Bridgwater docks. The wooden hatch-covers are shown on each side of the deck beside the bulwarks.

limited company, his cousin J.W. Sully jun, a younger son of the remaining founder, a director until his death in 1900. Thomas J. Sully, eldest son of Richard, joined the firm in 1893 and by 1903 was manager at Bridgwater.

During the First World War the firm was appointed by the Government to control the distribution of coal in the Somerset area. By 1921 the coal trade was deregulated and had reverted to private enterprise, but changed conditions, increased railway rates and dock charges seriously affected the transportation of coal by water. Practically the whole undertaking became rail-borne and Bridgwater as a port for the distribution of coal in the West Country almost ceased to exist.

On 12 January 1928 Richard Owen Sully died aged 78, leaving a wife, two sons and three daughters. On 10 June 1935 John George Sully died at Clevedon, aged 90, the last surviving son of James Wood Sully. He left a wife, seven sons and two daughters. Between 1935 and 1967 boats carrying the trademark of Sully & Co., a black funnel with white St George's cross, continued to berth at Sully's wharf on the south side of the outer or tidal basin of the docks. The wharf closed in 1967, although the vacant site continues to this day to be referred to as 'Sully's yard'.

The steeple of St Mary's church is just visible between the rigging of the schooner *Perriton*, built in 1881 on the beach at Minehead by Watchet shipbuilder Ben Williams for Thomas Kent Ridler of Minehead. She took eighteen months to construct and was the first ship built at Minehead since 1798. She was sunk on 29 January 1918 by gunfire from a German submarine, fortunately without loss of life.

A unique view of three double-ended Parrett barges riding the tidal bore at Crowpill, Bridgwater. The oar, or sweep as it was also known, was used as a rudder, or like a punt pole, to steady the craft. When the weather allowed a small square sail was occasionally set.

A nostalgic view of a pre-war steamship as she is manoeuvred through the narrow lock entrance to Bridgwater docks. The Holms Sand and Gravel Company's suction dredger *Sandholm* returning from the sandbanks of the Bristol Channel, having dredged up her cargo of 500–600 tons, would discharge it at the western end of the inner basin to the docks, while ships arriving at the quay alongside the dock and canal office near Dock Cottages would be booked in. The author remembers many a happy hour spent watching the employees of the dock company and the pilot exercising their skills in bringing the ships into the tidal dock with only inches to spare on either side.

An early photograph taken around 1865 of the schooner *Chard*, built at Bristol in 1844 and registered at Bridgwater in the same year. In May 1880, while carrying slate from Portmadoc to Southampton, the crew of this vessel, including Captain Jones of Highbridge, had to abandon ship, but they were rescued by the Norwegian barque *Tetens*. This photograph was taken before the construction of the Telescopic Bridge near Barhams Brickyard in 1871.

The Bascule Bridge, shown here with the Irish three-masted motor schooner *M.E. Johnstone* leaving the floating dock and entering the tidal basin for the River Parrett and the open sea.

GWR 0–4–0 pannier tank engine 1338, ex-Cardiff Railway, shunting alongside the Bridgwater docks in 1947. Railway lines surrounded the edge of the dock to Randle's Timberyard, Bowering's Animal Feeds and Sully's coal yards. In the background can be seen the hand-operated crane used for loading and off-loading vessels. The base plate to this crane is still in position at the western end of the inner basin.

The Canal and Docks, Bridgwater.

The masts of many ships moored in the Bridgwater docks reflect beautifully in the still waters of the canal at Newton Lock. The buildings to the left were erected in 1869, subsequently belonged to British Oil and Cake Mills and were later owned by Bowering's. On the extreme right is the 110 ft high kiln known as the 'Glass Cone' or the 'Glass House', originally used for firing glass but later converted for pottery. Built in 1771 by James Brydges, first Duke of Chandos, it was demolished in 1943, to provide the necessary hardcore for local airfields in wartime. The kiln base remained and has been preserved as an important example of industrial history. The two mile section of the Bridgwater to Taunton Canal from Huntworth to the floating harbour was not completed until 1841, to coincide with the opening of Bridgwater docks. Records show only 23 barges using the canal between 1905 and 1912; these carried sand, timber, coal and bricks.

The horse and cart of 'Gramp' Warren, pictured in the brickyard of H.J. Major & Co. Ltd in Colley Lane, Bridgwater.

The lock gates between the inner and outer docks at Bridgwater. The Dutch motor vessel *Saturnus* is discharging her cargo of 45 gallon drums of dried milk powder from Dublin. (The author remembers many happy hours with the crew of the *Saturnus*, who provided provisions during the austere years immediately after the war.) On the left is the converted gunboat 325 *Eidolon*, a 'C' class 110 ft long Fairmile. She was bought in 1947 by Peter Brett of Bridgwater and used as a home until he sold her in 1954.

A view along the river to the bridge and double-ended Parrett barges alongside Binford Place. The barges would carry up river towards Langport anything up to 14,000 bricks or twenty tons in weight and were often propelled by the long oar, or sweep. Alongside East and West Quays a number of sailing ships are moored, a familiar sight in those days. The barge in the foreground has the initials S.T.Co.Ltd. No. 2, indicating that it belongs to the Somerset Trading Co. The slipway to the stern of the barge was built in 1488 and known as 'Langport Slip' or 'New Slip'. Goods were transhipped here in order to continue their journey up or down the river. Bath bricks, believed to have been named after their resemblance in colour to Bath stone, were first manufactured locally in around 1823 from the slime or silt that had accumulated within the two mile length of the banks of the river between Somerset Bridge and Castle Fields. Companies sprang up to take advantage of the growing trade, and names like Barhams, Colthurst Symons, Parrett Bath Brick and John Board became part of the local scene. Slime dug from the River Parrett at low tide was mixed in a mill, rolled (called 'obstricking') and placed in rectangular moulds, then tapped out and placed on pallets (known as hacks) for drying. Once dry the bricks were put into an up-draught bottle-shaped kiln. After a short time they were wrapped for sale locally and for export to Europe, the Middle East, America and China. Millions were made annually and were used for cleaning and scouring. By the start of the Second World War the industry had almost ceased, as alternative cleaning methods became more popular.

The junction of East Quay, Eastover and Salmon Parade, Bridgwater, dominated by the YMCA building on the corner. Constructed on the site of the old Globe Hotel in 1887, and known as the George Williams Memorial Building, it was demolished in 1968 to make way for modern shop development. The square buildings situated on the quayside were built in 1868 and are toilet blocks. Moored nearest to the bridge is the trow *Nora*, owned by William Webb of Dunball and captained by William Britton of Bridgwater.

The River Parrett was well known for the hazards presented to shipping by the effects of harsh winters, as these pictures clearly show. Dangerous ice floes were not uncommon, and some years the river froze over completely. Some of the severest winters over the last 125 years have been 1870, 1880, 1887, 1895, 1907, 1917, 1933 (below), 1940 (above), 1947 and 1963.

The 1913 labour demonstration on Saturday 22 June brought men and women on to the streets of Bridgwater in a show of strength and protest. Organized by the Bridgwater branch of the National Union of Railwaymen, whose membership was 230, the procession included hundreds of dockers, shipwrights, tailors, insurance agents, shop assistants and members of the Co-operative movement. As the procession moved off from St John Street its numbers swelled to over 2,000 after it was joined by other union branches from Highbridge and Bath. Carrying banners displaying the words 'Success to our Cause', the protestors made their way to the Town Hall for one of the largest labour meetings in the area. Speaker after speaker echoed the causes of labour unrest which, to the anger of owners and managers in their turn, was resulting in loss of production.

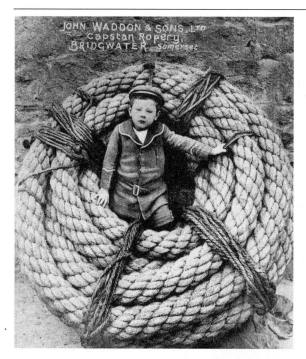

This fine advertisement postcard of John Waddon & Sons Ltd of Eastover, Bridgwater shows a typical massive core hawser, two feet in circumference. Known as 'junks', they were specially made by Waddon's for Watchet harbour, where they were used by the hobblers to moor the large steamers. The former site of these premises is now named Rope Walk.

Overlooking the River Parrett at West Quay, Bridgwater is this Norman watergate, the remains of the ancient Castle of Bridgwater originally built by William de Briwere during the reign of King John, in the thirteenth century, but destroyed by Fairfax and Cromwell after the siege in the seventeenth century.

With only one road bridge spanning the River Parrett between the estuary and Burrowbridge, it was inevitable that the Town Bridge at Bridgwater would become a bottleneck for traffic as the number of vehicles increased. On 29 March 1958 the long awaited internal bypass, known as Broadway, was opened with a second road crossing of the river. Blake Bridge, as it was to be known, had two 45 ft side spans with a 70 ft centre span constructed from reinforced concrete.

An unusual view from the top of the YMCA building, which stood on the corner of Eastover and Salmon Parade, looking over the rooftops of East Quay towards the drawbridge, a telescopic construction which took some fifteen months to build and was opened in 1871. To the right of the picture can be seen the masts of a ketch in the dry dock of Carver's Yard, with the brickyard kilns of Barhams in the distance.

On Wednesday 21 April 1938 Commander Graham of Stawell, accompanied by his daughter, set sail from Bridgwater docks in his 11 ton sailing boat *Caplin* on a voyage across the Atlantic. With an 8 hp auxiliary motor, the 34 ft craft sailed via the Azores, Bermuda and the West Indies, taking some twelve months to complete the voyage. Crowds lining the dockside to wish them 'bon voyage' included Bridgwater's mayor, Councillor W. Chard.

An early Severn trow *Gloster Packet* (Stroud, 1824), moored alongside the south side of Bridgwater's floating dock. The railway track which ran alongside the quay is clearly visible, together with the Chandos kiln on the premises of the Somerset Trading Company. Beyond the 'Gloster Packet' is the schooner *Little Mystery*, built at Kingsbridge in 1887, which was destroyed off the Isle of Wight in June 1917 by enemy gunfire.

The ketch *Fanny Jane*, built in 1858 by John Gough of Crowpill, Bridgwater, is firmly held by wooden poles in the dry dock of F.J. Carver at East Quay, Bridgwater. On the right of the picture can be seen the gang-plank providing access to the deck, the main and mizzen mast sails furled and coated, revealing the boom to the fore staysail, and the starboard bower anchor lowered to the dock floor while the port anchor hangs at the hawsepipe. The dock, built around 1740 and last used in 1942, had stepped sides, the supports being used to retain the vessel in an upright position after the water level had drained back out into the river. Sadly no remains of this dry dock are visible today.

The bow of the ketch *Sunshine* secure in dry dock.

The Town Bridge decorations celebrating the coronation of King George VI on 12 May 1937 are reflected here in the wet road. A vast amount of time, effort and imagination went into the spectacular decorations that adorned the town.

The annual July street procession in aid of Bridgwater Hospital Saturday Fund is seen here crossing Bridgwater's Town Bridge in 1910. Resplendent in gleaming livery, the carriages and well groomed horses pull their VIP occupants, while local fire officers on foot add further colour. This charity event always attracted large crowds willing to hand over pennies to swell the funds for such a worthy cause in the days long before the National Health Service.

A picture for posterity. Local brick and tile workers pose with the tools of their trade, a scene familiar until the Bridgwater yards dwindled and died. Even in the days of the Roman occupation, clay was taken from the River Parrett for making pottery, but it was not until the nineteenth century that brick and tile production became commercially viable. From then until the First World War the process flourished, with companies which included Colthurst Symons, Barham Bros. and John Board, to name a few, making a very important contribution to the economic and industrial development of Bridgwater. By 1861 manufacture ran at 8 million bricks per annum, increasing to 17 million by 1900, much going to the export market. But development of cheaper and more effective alternatives led to a trade downturn. Depletion of manpower and disruption of exports by the First World War added to the decline, and the industry was finally doomed by its inability to respond to the need for modern manufacturing processes and equipment. Use of the river and docks for both production and transportation dwindled.

The low roof-line of the Anchor public house and the furniture store of Ekers, next to the Kings Arms public house at West Quay, provide the background for this view of the Sully & Co. ketch *Good Templar*. Built in 1881 at Goole and registered at Bridgwater in 1895, she foundered off the Welsh Coast in November 1911, the mate losing his life. Laden with coal for the Bridgwater Gas Company, she lost her steering gear during a strong gale, her bulwarks were torn away, the vessel's small boat smashed and, finally, the mizzen sail was torn to ribbons. However, an approaching craft saw her distress signals and a steam trawler from Fleetwood in the vicinity took off Captain Creemer of Bristol Road, Bridgwater and the three remaining crew, the craft sinking stern first only a short while later.

Wednesday 5 June 1907 was a chill morning for the launch of the *Irene* from the slipway of Messrs F.J. Carver & Sons' shipbuilding yard at East Quay, Bridgwater. With a length of 85 ft, a breadth of 21 ft, and a depth of 9 ft, she was registered to carry 165 tons. Purchased by Clifford J. Symons of Taunton Road, Bridgwater, Clifford Symons of Camden Road, Bridgwater and Captain William Lee, her future skipper, she was used in general trade from the port of Bridgwater. As she slid into the river, the *Irene* drifted across the water to be moored alongside the Bridgwater ketch *Sunshine*. Alongside East Quay she was fitted out with masts, rigging, crew quarters and so on prior to her maiden voyage.

An artistic study of the steamship *Acra* alongside Saltlands as she is manoeuvered through the narrow entrance of Bridgwater docks. The bowsprit of another vessel is visible to the right, and a Sully's coal ship awaits her berthing on the high tide. This photograph, taken from a damaged glass plate, is worthy of inclusion, if only for its portrayal of the action necessary when a number of ships converged on the docks at the same time. Sailing ships were winched into the tidal basin using a pulley attached to the dockside.

The present Town Bridge was officially opened on 5 November 1883, replacing an earlier structure which proved too steep and inadequate. In this photograph the mayoress, Mrs W.T. Holland, having been brought to the centre of the bridge in a horse-drawn carriage, is shown unlocking a padlock attached to a brass chain suspended across the bridge centre underneath the flags. As the National Anthem was played, the mayoress led a procession, which included the band of the Rifle Corps, across the new bridge. In the evening a firework display, followed by the Guy Fawkes Procession, took place. This was only the second official Bridgwater Guy Fawkes Procession ever, but now, well over a century later, the event surpasses itself annually.

A civic inspection of the buoys strategically placed in the Bristol Channel for shipping using the River Parrett was carried out annually. Led by the mayor, members of the Corporation, magistrates and borough officials would board the steam tug *Bonita* with Captain Smart in charge. Leaving West Quay, the 12-hour, 120-mile trip would take in Lynmouth, the Welsh coast and the Devon and Somerset coasts. Catering facilities were provided by Taylor's of High Street, Bridgwater. A large crowd of townsfolk would congregate on the quay to welcome home the intrepid sailors, whose return would be signalled by the firing of a cannon. Are civic outings as exciting today?

The steamship *Crowpill* discharging coal alongside Sully's wharf in Bridgwater docks. In the foreground is the barge lock, only opened in recent years for the occasional motor boat or the flat barge used by divers for dock repairs. The docks now enjoy a new lease of life with the restoration and conversion of Ware's warehouse, the construction of an attractive apartment development and the re-opening of the canal. The barge lock, now restored, will be the main access for small craft entering or leaving the Parrett, but whether shipping will ever equal that of the past is very doubtful.

Sully & Co.'s ketch *Parkend* was moored for some years at this berth in Bridgwater docks. Built in 1873 at Ipswich, she was originally rigged as a brigantine and later re-rigged as a ketch, as shown here. Facing her is the iron steamship *Bulldog*, also owned by Sully & Co.

To the left of this picture is the schooner *North Barrule*, built at Ramsay in the Isle of Man in 1880 and named after a mountain called North Barrule just south of Ramsay. This was the earliest motorized cargo vessel to enter Bridgwater docks, her 21 hp auxiliary engine having been fitted in 1909. On her inside is the steamship *Devonia*, dressed overall with flags flying at the main and mizzen mast, with the *Irene* just visible behind. This photograph was taken on the occasion of the Silver Jubilee of King George V on 6 May 1935.

Built in 1932 for the Somerset Rivers Catchment Board, the 50 ft long *Persevere* was known as an hydraulic erosion dredger. With a hull built by Charles Hill of Bristol, and pumps and jets designed and built by W. & F. Wills of Bridgwater, this dredger used high velocity water jets which disturbed the silt along each side of the Parrett banks, which was then carried away by the flow of the tidal water to the open sea. The engine consisted of two 75 bhp three-cylinder Petter 'Atomic Diesel' marine engines, one for propulsion, the other for driving the six jets of the eroding plant, two of which pointed downwards while two inclined downwards at an angle of 12 degrees from the horizontal. A further submerged jet swivelled at the bow and the remaining jet swivelled on the deck for trimming the banks.

Looking across Bridgwater docks from the 'Mump' provides a superb view of the ketch *Sunshine* high in the water after unloading her cargo. Behind the railway trucks, to the right of this photograph taken in 1935, is the timberyard of George Randle & Son Ltd, and in the far distance can be seen the spire of St Mary's church with the brewery of Starkey, Knight & Ford Ltd at centre back of the picture.

The 'Mump', created from spoil accumulated from the excavations of Bridgwater dock between 1837 and 1840, is the backdrop to this photograph taken around 1930 of the steel topsail schooner *C.&F. Nurse*, owned and commanded by Captain Kelly of Nether Stowey. Both gaffs have been lowered to the main and mizzen boom ready for sailing. Alongside is the tugboat *Edward Batters* built in 1908 at South Shields but not registered at Bridgwater until 1922 and broken up in 1934.

The full length of the Somerset & Dorset Railway wharf is shown in this photograph taken from Saltlands towards the east bank of the Parrett at Bridgwater. A number of brick kilns, known locally as 'Pinnacle' kilns, is visible in the distance. On the left is the 1827 Brimscombe-built trow *Palace*, which became the subject of a rescue in April 1916 when she got into difficulties off Sand Point, Kewstoke Bay and three crew members and the ship's dog were rescued by the Weston-super-Mare lifeboat. To the right is the ketch *Stroud Packet*, built in 1823 also at Brimscombe (Gloucester). The trow with her side-cloths in position and the ketch with her hatch-covers fixed suggests that these two vessels were taking the next tide, having discharged their coal cargoes for owners George Bryant and Sons, coal merchants of Bridgwater.

George Sharman was captain of the *Robin Hood* on a voyage from Lydney to Bridgwater with a cargo of coal on 1 December 1909 when she went ashore and sank at the east point of the River Usk during a raging gale. All on board were rescued by the SS *Bulldog*, also from Bridgwater. Built in Bristol in 1852, this 39 ton trow is seen here alongside East Quay near the premises of F.J. Carver. She had an open hold, no hatches, and canvas side-cloths (visible and in position). Her mizzen boom appears to have been pulled up several feet to allow the crew to walk about at the stern.

The converted steam tug *Parret* passing through the moveable centre section of the telescopic bridge in 1949. The first boat through for some eleven years, the *Parret* was built at Queensferry in 1915 but not registered at Bridgwater until 1929 and broken up in 1959. On this occasion the telescopic bridge was manually withdrawn by an engineer summoned from Taunton, as the steam engine normally used to open the bridge was no longer working after so many years of inaction.

The trucks of Sully & Co. line the wharf of East Quay, Bridgwater on the south side of the Bascule Bridge, having been filled with coal brought from South Wales. Coal was discharged by hand into metal tubs, off-loaded by steam crane on to a wooden platform, then into the waiting coal wagons. The steamship *Welsh Prince* was built in 1871 by G.K. Stothert at Bristol but not registered at Bridgwater until 1904. Owned by Sully & Co., she was broken up in 1930.

A busy scene at Bridgwater docks, although the two lads seem more interested in the cameraman. From the left are the ketch *Crowpill*, the ketch *Parkend*, the dock-scraper *Bertha*, the ketch *Marie Eugine* and the three-masted topsail schooner *Circe*.

The rigging of a vessel alongside West Quay, Bridgwater forms a frame for this view of the schooner *Lilla* moored opposite. Built in 1868 at Freckleton, the *Lilla*, of 55 tons, was registered at Bridgwater in 1894 and traded until being hulked in 1928. In the background is the YMCA building. The hand-operated crane for loading and unloading ships remains to this day on the reconstructed East Quay.

This pre-war sand dredger belonging to the Bristol Sand & Gravel Company, *Dunkerton*, is pictured alongside the firm's wharf, then visible beside the main A38 Bristol road. The land for this wharf was purchased in May 1935 to facilitate the unloading of materials connected with the construction of the British Cellophane factory in Bath Road, Bridgwater. The author's house, from where he spent many happy hours watching the boats coming up and down the Parrett and the discharging of sand and gravel at this wharf, was to the left of this picture.

A photograph illustrating clearly the timber planking of the stern of the Bridgwater-built ketch *Fanny Jane*, moored alongside railway wagons on the south side of the inner dock at Bridgwater. Railway lines ran along three sides of the floating dock, small turn-tables enabling railway trucks to be turned by 90 degrees so as to serve each side of the dock for loading and unloading purposes. In the background is the hopper of the Holms Sand & Gravel Co., where the sand dredgers of the company would discharge their sand and gravel.

Robert Blake was born in 1598 in a stone property in Blake Street, formerly St Mary Street, Bridgwater. The eldest of the fourteen children of Humphrey Blake, an export merchant of substance, the grandson and son of local mayors of Bridgwater, he spent the first sixteen years of his life at home adjacent to the River Parrett and Durleigh Brook and within sight of the old stone bridge. Following some nine years at Oxford, he returned to the area, living at Knowle Manor, Puriton (now demolished), overlooking Downend Pylle and the loop in the River Parrett. (This loop existed until 1678 when Sir John Moulton completed his plan to straighten the river at Viking's Pill on Horsey Level, thereby reclaiming some 150 acres of land and easing the difficulties of wind-assisted sailing ships in navigating to Bridgwater.)

The naval and historical successes of Robert Blake have been documented at length elsewhere, and brief reference here to this hero and son of Bridgwater is a mark of respect and regard for the town's most famous man.

The famous three-masted schooner *Kathleen & May* alongside the wharf of the Parrett Bath Brick Co. Built in 1900 at Connah's Quay, Flintshire by Ferguson & Baird, she is now preserved by the Maritime Trust at St Katharine's Dock, London. The Bristol Road premises of the Parrett Bath Brick Co. concentrated on the production of Bath bricks from 1886 and continued right up to the outbreak of war in 1939. To the left are the chimney pots of Parrett Buildings alongside the A38 into Bridgwater.

Bridgwater's *Irene* alongside the Bristol Road premises of the Parrett Bath Brick Co. To the left of the bowsprit is the newly constructed chimney of British Cellophane, now known as Courtaulds. By virtue of her longevity and restoration as a historical sailing ship, the *Irene* may have acquired an importance her builders and subsequent owners could not have imagined.

Between the masts of the *Irene* can be seen the steam crane built by Thomas Smith of Rodley near Leeds. The crane ran on broad gauge track along the 400 ft wharf of the Somerset & Dorset Joint Railway on the east bank of the River Parrett at Bridgwater. Staging below the bowsprit suggests the *Irene* was undergoing the final painting of her hull after being fitted out with masts, rigging and crew quarters following her launch on 5 June 1907. The flags decorating her mainmast may have heralded her maiden voyage.

The brickyard of Colthurst Symons provides the backcloth for this photograph of the ketch *Two Brothers*, built originally as a trow by John Gough of Bridgwater and broken up in 1922. Bath bricks were produced by Colthurst Symons on the Bristol Road site from about 1861 and advertised as late as 1939, although by then the demise of the industry was imminent, the competition from alternative cleaning agents proving too great.

On Tuesday 28 June 1927 the German steamship *Masuren*, bringing a cargo of 500–600 tons of timber for the Somerset Trading Co., ran aground on the western bank at Saltlands on a two foot ebb tide. Listing heavily to port, she straddled the river, keeling over and finally capsizing on her side with her funnel practically parallel with the water. The pilot and crew escaped along the mast to the eastern bank. As she filled with water her cargo was thrown overboard and floated upstream. After her deck cargo was eventually removed and the holds pumped out the incoming tide righted her so that she could be safely moored on the west bank.

The western end of the docks, with the premises of Holms Sand & Gravel Co. Ltd and the timberyard of Geo. Randle & Son Ltd to the left. Sand dredgers using suction pumps brought up 'Bristol Channel' grit, 'Holms' sand and 'Bideford' gravel from the bed of the Bristol Channel, which was then unloaded at this wharf by crane into hoppers before being distributed by road transport.

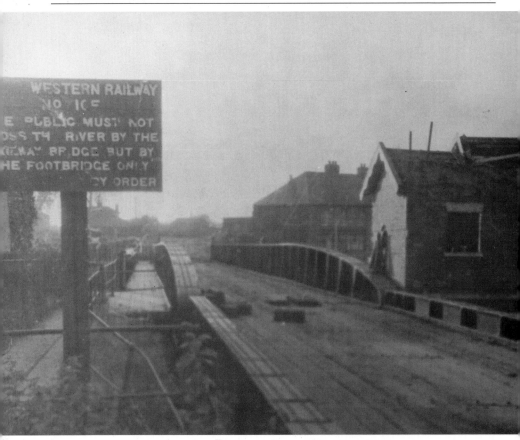

The old iron single-track rail bridge seen here in about 1969 is in a rather sad state of disrepair, the steam engine in the machine house to the right having been removed by British Railways in the early 1960s. The heavy wooden planking was removed in 1982 when the bridge was converted for road traffic use. On the brickwork some three feet higher than the river bank is a flood mark dated 1883. Completed in March 1871, the telescopic bridge, or 'black bridge' as it was known locally, consisted of three sections. A cog mechanism in the engine house, powered by a steam engine with a vertical boiler, pulled the traverser section sidewards into the traverser pit. This allowed the balanced middle section of the bridge to be rolled back by the chains attached half-way along the underside of this section into the area vacated by the traverser. The third section of the bridge was fixed between the west bank and supporting pillars in the river. In the event of engine failure it was possible for the bridge to be opened and closed by manually operated winches.

The bows of the Sully-owned steamships *Parret* and *Crowpill*, easily distinguished by the white upright cross upon a black background on their funnel. Across the docks are the premises of the British Oil and Cake Mills, later to become Bowering's, manufacturers of animal feeding stuffs, a familiar landmark to this day. On the left is one of the two steam cranes which travelled on standard gauge track along the south side of the floating dock.

In 1895 the River Parrett froze over in one of the coldest winters ever known. A bonfire has been lit on the ice, while crowds of onlookers watch from the bridge. Photographs of this unusual sight were in great demand and sold quickly as local people sought a permanent record of an unusual event.

This early view is believed to show 'hobblers' congregating at West Quay. 'Hobblers' were casual workers from the area, taken on when ships were mooring or casting off, who did the routine but hard work of lowering or hoisting sails, securing, releasing and storing mooring ropes and raising and lowering anchors to winch the vessel alongside the berth, a procedure known as 'warping' or 'tracking'. Competition between the men for work was fierce and they would hang around all day hoping for a ship to employ them. A hobbler's fee was based upon the tonnage of the vessel and its country of origin, the heavier the tonnage, the harder and longer the job, and some owners were prepared to pay more for a speedier job. The lamp to the right was situated at the approach to the narrow and steep old Town Bridge which was demolished in 1883.

The 120 ton steamship *Parret* tied up alongside the premises of Messrs Peace Ltd at West Quay, Bridgwater in 1949. Her own steam-driven derrick was used for unloading sacks of flour on to a waiting lorry. The hatch beams are shown being inserted into position before the covers are fitted prior to sailing. This proved to be a historic photograph, since it shows the last ship moored alongside either East or West Quay with cargo. The vessel was broken up in 1959.

Many local people will remember the three faithful steamships owned by Sully & Co. which plied their trade up and down the River Parrett, and which are shown here moored in the small tidal basin at Bridgwater. Nearest the camera is the *Crowpill*, built at South Shields in 1911 and broken up in 1966, then the *Parret*, built at Queensferry in 1915 and broken up in 1959, and on her inside *Enid*, built in Maryhill, Lanark and also broken up in 1959.

The beautiful 1795 iron bridge with a 75 ft span, cast by the Coalbrookdale Company of Shropshire, replaced the medieval Town Bridge at a cost of £4,000. The cast iron was brought to Bridgwater by trow via the River Severn. Affixed to the bridge after construction was a plaque bearing the name of Robert Codrington, mayor of Bridgwater in 1795. The increase in horse-drawn traffic, which had to take the steep incline each side of the bridge at slow speed and with extreme care, soon caused traffic problems and the need for a replacement bridge became urgent.

The steam paddle-tug *Petrel*, built at Low Walker in 1863 and owned by Sully & Co., moored alongside the premises of Carver & Sons, shipbuilders of East Quay, Bridgwater. These paddle-tugs were used to tow several sailing vessels roped together in line to and from the mouth of the Parrett estuary as high tide approached.

Young men pose on the ice beneath the paddle wheel during the hard winter of 1880.

Mr William Pocock at Valetta Place, Bridgwater, with his salmon net and two fine specimens of locally caught fish. The net comprised an ash pole called a 'spill', some 10 ft long, with two curved willow stays of about 4½ ft divided by a two-holed yoke fixed to the spill, covered with a net with a two-inch mesh. It was illegal for salmon to be taken from the river with a net between the hours of 6 a.m. on Saturday and 6 a.m. on Monday, unless a rod or salmon butt was used. The butt was a basket made from local withies laid in rows on the muddy bank and was the favoured form of salmon fishing towards the mouth of the river.

In 1874 a gridiron, a 162 ft long heavy timber construction, was set down alongside East Quay to enable vessels to be serviced, maintained or repaired. The ketch *Galley* rests upon timbers alongside the premises of F.J. Carver & Son Ltd at low tide, with the stern of Sully & Co.'s steamship *Welsh Prince* visible to the right.

A foreign motor vessel discharging her cargo directly into trucks on the quay, alongside Ware's Warehouse.

The unique double-leaf Bascule Bridge opened manually to allow the Sully-owned steamship *Parret* passage to the inner basin in order to discharge her cargo at Bridgwater docks in 1952. In 1977 this bridge was closed to traffic and a temporary structure built for traffic going to Chilton Trinity. In 1981 the bridge was removed and a specialist Derby company restored the structure to its original condition. In 1983 each 30 ton section was reinstalled on its bearings and the winding-gear was connected up.

Shipping moored alongside both East and West Quays, the hook of the hand-operated crane used for loading and unloading vessels securely held by a fixed ring in the quayside. To the right is Wilkinson and Leng's hardware store and builders merchants. The property with the porch next door was the post office until 1870, when this was transferred to High Street before being moved to the Cornhill in 1909.

This travelling steam crane, built by Thomas Smith of Leeds, moved on broad gauge track along the 255 ft timber wharf of the Somerset & Dorset Joint Railway landing stage situated between Barham's brickyard and Colthurst Symons' premises on the east bank of the River Parrett at Bridgwater. In 1912 the wooden structure became so dilapidated that the area was fenced off and by 1920 the crane had been transferred under its own steam to Highbridge wharf, where it continued its life loading and unloading ships belonging to the S&DJR. The crane driver had no overhead protection and had to endure whatever weather conditions prevailed.

The unladen Bridgwater-built ketch *New Design* alongside the wooden staging of Barhams, East Quay, Bridgwater. A mobile steam crane with galvanized weather protection stands by to load bricks and tiles. Little of this staging is now visible as time and tide have taken their toll on the timber construction. The several buckets on the quay in front of the crane suggest coal was unloaded, although they may have been used to discharge sand, stone or lime. In her latter years the ketch was laid up at Bristol Bridge and finally hulked in 1951.

A bleak wintertime view of the Town Bridge and river.

The Great Western Railway Company dock dredger *Bertha*, believed to have been designed by Brunel in 1844 and now regarded as the oldest operating steam craft in Britain and possibly the world. Preserved and on show at Exeter Maritime Museum, the dredger pulled herself backwards and forwards across the dock on chains attached to the walls of the quayside. A large blade beneath the boat scraped and stirred the mud and silt, which was then sluiced from the basin into the river. The boiler needed many shovels of coal to build up enough steam for the pistons to produce the necessary 40 lb per square inch pressure. As much as half a ton of coal would be consumed in a full working day.

Employees of F.J. Carver & Son Ltd pose proudly for the camera of L. Slocombe while standing on the newly completed lockgate for the Clyce at Highbridge. On the reverse of this photographic postcard taken in 1926 Albert Paice writes that the gates 'took an average 3–4 weeks each to build. Each gate went in with absolutely no trouble without the least bit of trimming off the mitres' and he identified, from left to right: A.G. Attwell (manager), J. Trunks (yard handyman), B. Brightwell, A.E. Paice (blacksmith), C. Lewis (shipwright), W. Shakespear (shipwright), A. Paice (junior shipwright), S. King (shipwright), W.J. Blackmore (shipwright).

The Sully & Co. steamship *Crowpill* sitting high in the water with empty hold at Bridgwater docks in 1938. Built in 1911 at South Shields, she plied regularly with coal between Bridgwater and various South Wales ports during the period 1934 to 1966, when she was finally broken up. To her stern is the steamship *Enid*, built in 1903 at Maryhill, Lanark and also owned by Sully & Co. between 1931 and 1959, when she too was broken up. On her inside is the wooden steamer *Tender*, built by John Gough of Crowpill, Bridgwater in 1874 and used by Sully & Co. throughout her lifetime until she also met the fate of the ship-breaking gangs in 1943. Just visible in the distance are the ketches *Sunshine* and *Trio*. In 1873 the Port of Bridgwater ranked fifth in England for the importation of coal and culm (coal dust).

The fine two-masted topsail schooner *C.&F. Nurse*, built by Lean of Falmouth, moored alongside the starboard of the ketch *Fanny Jane*. The *C.&F. Nurse* sailed regularly between Bridgwater and the Mersey with Bath bricks, Runcorn and Fowey with coal, Fowey and London with China Clay, and thence back to Bridgwater with cement. She was later converted into a towing barge with the name *Enterprise* and used on the Gloucester Canal until hulked at Sharpness in 1936.

Masts, spars and bowsprits laced with rigging. The 276 ton *Ausgar* of Marstal, built in 1893, is to the left, moored alongside the 200 ton *Cimbria* of Troeuse, built at Svenborg in 1903. How magnificent these ships must have looked alongside each other!

The 69 ton ketch *Ade* (formerly *Annie Christian*) slipping her moorings in the tidal basin before sailing to Glasgow in 1912. Built as a schooner in Barnstaple in 1881 by William Westacott, she was beautifully decorated with scroll work below her bowsprit, a well-known trademark of this Devon builder. In 1888 she was sunk in a collision, but was refloated and re-rigged as a ketch. During the First World War she was fitted with a gun and motorized. Surviving war hostilities and storms, she saw 65 years' service before being broken up in 1946. In the background is Russell Place, a terrace of seven cottages and two higher grade houses decorated with local tiles. Built for dock workers, these dwellings flooded regularly until improved drainage in recent years solved the problem.

Built at Plymouth in 1790 from oak salvaged from an old British man-of-war of the George III period, the Bridgwater-registered ketch *Good Intent* is seen here alongside the quay at Bridgwater docks taking on cargo. In 1918 she was believed to be the oldest British merchant vessel afloat in the mercantile marine. In the ownership of the Smart family of Bridgwater for over fifty years, she regularly plied general goods between Bridgwater and Cardiff. In 1918 she was sold in Cardiff to Captain Bride for £385 and was scrapped at Pill around 1927. On her stern and taffrail were the words 'The Sea is His and He made it.' In the background can be seen the smithy.

Nineteenth-century sailors said that at times it was possible to cross the 200 ft width of the docks by walking over the decks of ships, so great were the numbers moored. While this picture does not show such a crossing as possible, it does illustrate the extent of shipping when at its peak in the late nineteenth century. Here are some twelve ships loading or unloading at the same time. They include the schooner *Sarah Jane*, the barque *Bertha* of Tomberg, Norway (built in Altona in 1865), the *Elbe* of Korpo, Finland (built in 1903), the *Maerdor*, the ketch *Industry*, the tug *Victor*, the schooner *Pique-au-Vent*, the *Arona* (built in Oskarshamn, Sweden in 1904), the ketch *Parkend*, the *Aldebaran*, and the ketch *Crowpill* (ex-*John Wesley*), built in Harwich in 1873.

In 1935 excavations were commenced for the construction of a new factory at Bath Road which was to be called British Cellophane, nowadays a subsidiary of Courtaulds. Taking the initiative, the Bristol Sand and Gravel Company purchased riverside land to develop wharves alongside the A38 Bristol Road so that building materials for the factory site could be brought up river cheaply and easily. With the completion of the factory, the wharves were used to discharge sand and gravel sucked from the bed of the Bristol Channel by sand dredgers as described elsewhere. This shows the discharging crane, sand hoppers and lorries being loaded with sand and gravel. The crane and hoppers have only recently disappeared, leaving the wharf with the rails of the mobile crane still in place today.

CARVER & SON, LTD
BRIDGWATER.

LENGTH OF DOCK – 104 F
WIDTH AT ENTRANCE – 24 F

Francis James Carver was the head of the shipbuilding firm of F.J. Carver & Son. Born in Chilton Trinity in 1836, he was apprenticed at John Gough's shipbuilding yard, then located on the western side of the Parrett just below the docks. After rising to foreman he started his own shipbuilding business on East Quay in about 1878, assisted by his son Frank who continued the business until his death in 1921. The company built many vessels in Bridgwater and its designs were much respected by Bristol Channel shipowners. Second son Harry was the managing director of the Bridgwater Motor Company, a firm of which he was co-founder in 1887 with premises at East Quay and later in Eastover, Bridgwater.

Registered at Bridgwater in 1903 but built at Milford in 1874, the 76 ton *Ermenilda* was the first locally registered ship to fall victim to the Germans when she was sunk on 4 August 1916 by a bomb in the English Channel while owned and captained by H. Hamblin of Gordon Terrace, Bridgwater and carrying a cargo of stone. A German submarine ordered the ship to be cleared within five minutes, the crew of four, including Mr Bailey and Mr Perks of Bridgwater, taking to a small boat which was cast adrift. A bomb placed on the forecastle was detonated by a time-fuse and the *Ermenilda* sank within ten minutes. After two hours of aimless drifting, the crew were picked up by a Russian steamer twenty-five miles off Portland and taken to Weymouth. This picture shows the *Ermenilda* alongside Ware's Warehouse at Bridgwater docks with the British Oil and Cake Mills in the background.

Another steamship owned by Sully & Co., the *Borderdene*, is seen here unloading coal brought from South Wales to the firm's wharf in Bridgwater docks in 1939. Built at Namur in 1913, this 122 ton vessel was mined in January 1942.

Captain James Lovell of Watchet was the master of the *Charles*, a schooner built in Bridgwater in 1857. On 18 December 1917 Captain Lovell was taken prisoner when this vessel was sunk by a German submarine in the English Channel, his mate being killed and two of his crew captured. This photograph of the ill-fated *Charles* was taken alongside the Bristol Road wharf which was acquired in 1922 by John Board & Company. This firm had been established in 1844 and had other premises at Dunball and Dunwear.

Low tide allows the employees of Carver & Son to caulk the hull of this 1884 schooner *Kings Oak*. Caulking was the packing of the joints and the stopping up of gaps between the planks of the hull with hemp strands driven into the seams with irons and mallets. Sometimes the fibre was impregnated with tar, or pitch was applied to the seams. Planks suspended by ropes along the side of the hull allowed the caulkers to work on the seams. The *Kings Oak* sank at Swansea in 1923 after failing to rise on the tide while sheltering from heavy weather on a journey from Liverpool to Bridgwater with a cargo of coal. During the storm a seaman named Robert Snell of Mount Street, Bridgwater drowned. The vessel was refloated, and repaired, and continued to trade before being broken up at Appledore, North Devon later in the same year.

In the foreground is the *RKP*, a 67 ton schooner built at Feock, Cornwall in 1870 and registered at Bridgwater in 1890. Partly owned by Edward Hamblin of Bridgwater and captained by Charles Hamblin, a brother, this graceful looking vessel went down with a 120 ton cargo of loose fish-curing salt en route from Gloucester to Bantry, Ireland on 29 October 1910.

The two-masted, single-topsail schooner *Lilla* loaded with bricks and tiles alongside the brickyard of Colthurst Symons. With high tide imminent her fore canvas topsail would be set on the upper yard and her journey down river would begin. Built in 1868 at Freckleton, she was registered at Bridgwater in 1894 and hulked in 1928.

The *Trio* was built in Jersey in 1877 and originally named *Warinula*, later changed to *Margherita*. Built as a schooner and later re-rigged as a ketch, her mizzen mast was fashioned from the timber of her old mainmast. Prior to her ownership in 1895 by the Escotts of Watchet, she was used in the Newfoundland cod trade. She is pictured here at Bridgwater docks while in the ownership of Captain Joseph Warren of Bridgwater but after 1927, when an auxiliary motor was fitted. She capsized in the Parrett in March 1939. On the right is the ketch *Sunshine*, built by Charles Burt of Falmouth in 1900 but owned by Captain Lewis Nurse of Bridgwater. Below her bowsprit the *Sunshine* carried the beautiful figurehead of a full-length figure of a woman in a broadbrimmed hat, shown here in close-up. In early December 1937, while bound for Dublin from Bridgwater, this 99 ton vessel grounded heavily near the eastern breakwater of Fishguard in high seas, and after sending out distress signals three crew members had to be rescued by the local lifeboat.

SECTION EIGHT
Upper Reaches

This double-ended Parrett barge loaded with bricks and tiles is shown alongside the Somerset Bridge works, whence the cargo would be taken into Bridgwater and there transferred to a sea-going ketch for onward transmission to all corners of the British Empire. With the advent of railways between the towns there was a rapid decline of exports from Bridgwater docks and from the wharves of the Parrett which had been used for centuries. By failing to take account of new technology, alternative building products and means of manufacture, the brickyards let the clay industry of the area fade and then fail.

In the hamlet of Somerset Bridge a river crossing for the Bristol & Exeter Railway Company was constructed. The young but already celebrated engineer Isambard Kingdom Brunel started work on the bridge in 1839. A centering constructed to support the arch was not removed until 1843, but there was a shift in the foundations and Brunel was required to design a replacement span. It is this replacement span, constructed of laminated timbers, that is shown here. By 1904 the replacement bridge of steel girders which remains to this day was in place.

Designed and built by W. & F. Wills Ltd of Bridgwater for the Somerset Drainage Commissioners in 1894, this hydraulic eroder named *Pioneer* used its high pressure water hoses to clear shoals from the bed of the river and accumulated silt from the river banks. This picture appears to have been taken upstream from Burrowbridge in around 1905.

The 62 ft steel-built steam scourer *Eroder* designed by Frank Wills of Bridgwater uses a Leval 110 hp turbine powering centrifugal pumps to clear the build-up of mud and silt along the Parrett banks. The pumps used 1,400 gallons per minute at 70 lb per square inch. Three men were required to operate the vessel.

The great freeze of February 1895 brought distress and disaster to many local families. Soup kitchens were set up, as well as a distress relief fund, so that local residents could obtain food supplies. In the midst of such winter hardship there was some light relief, however. Tea parties were held, for example, when fried pancakes were cooked over a brazier on the solid ice of the Parrett, in this instance at Moorland (Northmoor Green).

The confluence of the River Tone and River Parrett, some 200 yd to the south of Burrowbridge. The Tone joins at right angles from a south-westerly direction.

Burrowbridge. During the seventeenth century barges of up to fifteen tons made their way from here to Ham Mills, some three miles from Taunton, carrying coal and other goods. By the early part of the nineteenth century over 14,000 tons of cargo each year were brought into Taunton on the Parrett and Tone. In 1827 the opening of the Huntworth to Taunton Canal led to fierce competition between the Tone Conservators and the Management Committee of the Canal Company, but an agreement was reached in 1832. Two further canals linked in with Taunton: the Chard to Creech St Michael Canal, which opened in 1842, and the Grand Western Canal from Tiverton to Firepool, Taunton, opened in 1838.

For hundreds of years the drainage of the Somerset levels has been vital for agricultural and social reasons, and as far back as the thirteenth century the monks constructed ditches and banks to protect the levels from flooding. Between 1770 and 1825 extensive attempts were made to drain the levels, including the construction of the King's Sedgemoor Drain and its associated ditches and rhines. By 1830 Somerset had introduced its first steam pumping station at Westonzoyland, capable of lifting water from the levels and discharging it into the River Parrett. The original beam engine proved inadequate, and in 1861 a more successful centrifugal pump by Easton & Amos was placed in position. It remained in use until 1951. Now of historical significance and preserved by enthusiasts, this engine is fired regularly and can be viewed by the public on certain open days.

The A361 Taunton to Street road crosses the River Parrett at Burrowbridge at a point overlooked by Burrow Mump, which is surmounted by St Michael's chapel. The bridge, with its granite arch and parapet, was built in 1825 from blue lias blocks. The round aperture on each side of the arch allowed floodwater to drain away.

The toll-gate and toll-house on the river bridge, viewed from the Othery side. The tollkeeper, his wife, child and small dog are posing proudly for the photographer. The signboard set out all the relevant tolls. The right to use public roads free of toll having once been a strong political issue, it is interesting that all these years later tolls may well become a feature of future travel.

The River Parrett is well known for its elvers, Burrowbridge and Dunball being the favourite locations with local fishermen. The locally made net was designed on an 18 in frame covered with fine mesh which was held in place by two bent withies crossing from each corner. The elvers, usually caught at night during February and March, were transparent, some two to three inches long and the diameter of a matchstick. They were scooped out of the river then packed in boxes to be sent to local hotels and restaurants as well as to London and other gastronomic centres.

Towards the end of the last century the upper reaches were navigable, horse-drawn barges taking the coal brought into Bridgwater by ketch from Bristol and South Wales up river towards Langport and the wharves along the tributaries which constituted what became known as the upper reaches. On the outgoing tide goods were taken back to Bridgwater for transfer to seagoing craft. Not only could the barge horses jump fences while towing; they could also jump on to the deck of the barge when it was necessary to pole to the opposite river bank. The last barge to Burrowbridge was logged in 1928 and the last barge as far as Langport in 1910, although barges carrying withies passed through in the 1940s.

In 1821 an Act of Parliament created a body of commissioners empowered to demolish the old bridge and construct a new one, for which £2,500 had to be raised by the issue of £50 bonds taken up by local residents. Construction took place in 1825 and in 1828 tolls raised £146, but the railways took over and by 1883 income had dropped to £41. The introduction and popularity of the motor vehicle led to a resurgence of road use, and by 1921 the income from tolls had risen to £252 and by 1925 to £513, all from the 3d payable to the gatekeeper. Burrowbridge was the last toll-bridge in Somerset and was not 'freed' until 1946. The comic postcard shown here was published around 1912, and makes wry fun of the section of the original Act which stated 'for every horse, mule or ass drawing, 3d'.

At 3 a.m. on Saturday 7 December 1929, following unprecedented rainfall and high winds throughout the preceding fortnight, the River Tone burst its banks at Athelney. The breach occurred on the property of Mrs Miller at Stanmore, where the embankment separated the Tone from the low-lying lands of Stanmoor, King's Sedgemoor, West Sedgemoor, Aller Moor and the moors above Langport. The villages of Athelney, Stathe, Stoke St Gregory and Burrowbridge were devastated and the withy beds badly damaged, as were hayricks, farming implements, property and furniture. Poultry and livestock were lost, but, fortunately, there was no loss of life. A county relief fund was started, to relieve the hardship and distress to the community, as insurance failed to cover loss by 'Act of God'. It took many weeks for the waters to recede and even longer for the life in the community to return to normal. Indeed, some would say the floods changed attitudes and marked the turning point between the 'old days' and what followed, as new ideas and practices were introduced to prevent another disaster on the same scale, not all of which found favour.

Langport

Bow Bridge, Langport, photographed from the air in around 1933. The lock-house, office and floodgate are in the top left-hand corner. This three-arched bridge was built of Pilsbury stone in 1839 at a cost of £3,989. It replaced a nine-arched bridge, each arch of which had been so narrow only barges up to seven tons could pass through. (In 1800 a tramway had been built to hoist barges up to twenty tons over the old bridge.) The centre arch of the new bridge, larger than those either side, allowed bigger barges easy passage. Messrs Stuckey and Bagehot formed the Parrett Navigation Company, and at a cost of £38,000 constructed a canal to Westport with a series of locks that enabled the large 20 ton barges to get even further inland. By the 1850s almost 170,000 tons of cargo a year was passing through Langport. However, the advent of the railways and the introduction of bulk transportation resulted in river-borne carriage diminishing.

An early sketch of the nine-arched stone bridge across the River Parrett at Langport. Only cargo up to seven tons could pass through the narrow arches and anything over that had to be transferred to smaller craft before being taken up river.

Ice flows against Langport Bridge in the late 1930s. The new Bow Bridge at Langport was built with jutting keystones in 1839 to replace the old bridge. The central and larger of the three arches enabled cargo up to twenty tons to pass through, although the absence of a towpath required the horses to be unhitched on one side and re-attached on the other.

The new Bow Bridge at Langport opened up the prospect of moving cargo as far as Ilminster. The local families of Stuckey and Bagehot formed the Parrett Navigation Company and proceeded to cut the canal from Midelney to Westport, thus linking the Parrett with the Isle, whence a short journey by road took the cargo right into Ilminster and on to Chard. The families of Stuckey and Bagehot had been well known partners in the multiple share ownership of trading vessels as far back as 1707. Trading between local ports and South Wales in garden produce, bricks and tiles, as well as other items from local industry, they brought into Somerset coal, factory goods and indeed passengers. By the late 1820s they had shares in much larger sailing ships, usually 400 ton barques plying overseas and trading in Canada and the East Indies. The canal was open by 1841, and by the 1850s over 170,000 tons of cargo a year was passing through Langport, but the success of the venture was somewhat short-lived, with the opening of the rail link to Taunton, Langport and Yeovil in 1853. By 1910 only one barge was operating on the River Parrett between Langport and Bridgwater.

Little appears to be recorded of Langport as a shipbuilding town, but it has the distinction of having constructed at least one vessel, listed in Lloyds Register as the trow *Thorney*, in 1847. While it seems improbable that a 65 ton trow could have floated in the upper Parrett, unless the 'stream' was deeper in those days, records show that this open-hold vessel with canvas side-cloths, typical of these undecked trows, was indeed launched. The *Thorney* was captained in the 1880s by George Trunks of Williton and later by Captain Johnson. Registered at Bridgwater in 1849 and owned by Messrs Sully & Co., she ran aground in 1890 but was refloated. Her luck ran out on Saturday 23 August 1902, however, when she was involved in a collision with the ketch *New Design* near Bridgwater docks while laden with coal. The bill of her own anchor pierced her bow and she sank rapidly. At low tide two barges of coal were removed from her hold, her leak was stopped, and she was floated to the outer basin of the docks, but in such a dilapidated condition that she had to be hulked. The *Thorney* is pictured on the extreme right of this photograph taken at Ilfracombe in around 1890.

Bibliography

Anderson, J., *Coastwise Sail*, Percival Marshall, 1948.
Bouguet, M., *West Country Sail; Merchant Shipping, 1840–1960*, David & Charles, 1971.
Bridgwater Mercury (1870–1970).
Eglinton, E., *The Last of the Sailing Coasters*, London, 1982.
Farr, G., *Somerset Harbours*, Christopher Johnson, 1954.
Farr, G., *West Country Passenger Steamers*, T. Stephenson, 1967.
Farr, G., *Ships and Harbours of Exmoor*, Microstudies, 1970.
Farr, G., *Wreck and Rescue in the Bristol Channel*, Vol. 1, Bradford Barton, 1966.
Farr, G., papers for *Somerset Maritime History*, 1979, Somerset Record Office.
Greenhill, B., *The Merchant Schooners*, Conway Maritime Press, 1988.
Harrison, J.D., *The Bridgwater Railway*, Oakwood Press, 1990.
Mote, G., *The Westcountrymen*, Badger Books, 1986.
Murless, B.J., 'The Bath Brick Industry of Bridgwater', *Jnl. Som. Ind. Arch. Soc.*, No. 1 (1975) 18–28.
Murless, B.J., *Bridgwater Docks and the River Parrett*, Somerset County Library, 1983.
Norman, B., *Tales of Watchet Harbour*, 1985.
Porter, E., *Bridgwater Industries Past and Present*, Purnell, undated.
Shaw, A., 'The Bridgwater Flatner', *Mariner's Mirror*, Vol. 55 (1969), 411–15.
Slade, W.J., *Out of Appledore*, Conway Maritime, 1972.
Slade, W.J. & Greenhill, B., *West Country Coasting Ketches*, Conway Maritime, 1974.

Acknowledgements

The production of this book would not have been possible without the assistance of others, and the author is indebted to everyone who gave information, help and encouragement, including: Mr D. Blackhurst (Salcombe), Mr P. Brett (Poole), Mrs Heather Cavell (Burnham-on-Sea), Mr Nick Chipchase (Taunton), Mr & Mrs C.H. Conelley (Pawlett), Mr Nigel Coombes (Portishead), Mr C. Franks (Holford), Miss E. Harris (Puriton), Mr John Lamb (West Huntspill), Mr Will Lock (Bridgwater), the late Mrs Lilly Male (Isle Brewers), Mr Brian Murless (Taunton), the North Devon Maritime Museum at Appledore, Mr George Owen, Mrs A.G. Parish (Walpole), Mrs M.A. Peek (Woolavington), Mrs S. Weatherhead (Pawlett), J. Weston (Gwent). Thanks are due to Mrs L. Luke of Edithmead, who entrusted the author with the wonderful collection of photographs amassed by her late husband, Ivor, and to the late Gilbert Young for invaluable information. Grateful thanks are accorded to good friend Will Loudon, whose encouragement and enthusiasm never wains and Richard Storey of Kenilworth, who undertook the proof-reading. No book is ever completed without the help and patience of one's family and my wife Celia was totally supportive throughout.

Only a handful of vessels referred to in this publication still exist, the rest are history, and only photographs can re-create the River Parrett's heritage and suggest its importance in bringing trade, employment and affluence to the ports along its length and tributaries.

While every effort has been made to ensure the accuracy of the facts contained in this publication, memories do fade, recollections falter, and original documentation is sometimes illegible. Apologies are offered for any accidental or unintentional mistakes. Indeed, any further information on the subjects covered, corrections, or details of personal experiences would be most welcome and much appreciated. The author may be contacted by writing to 11 Regency Drive, Green Lane, Coventry, CV3 6QA. It is hoped that this book gives pleasure to those who enjoy recollecting the nostalgic past of sail and steam, ship and shipmaster, pill and port, coast and river.